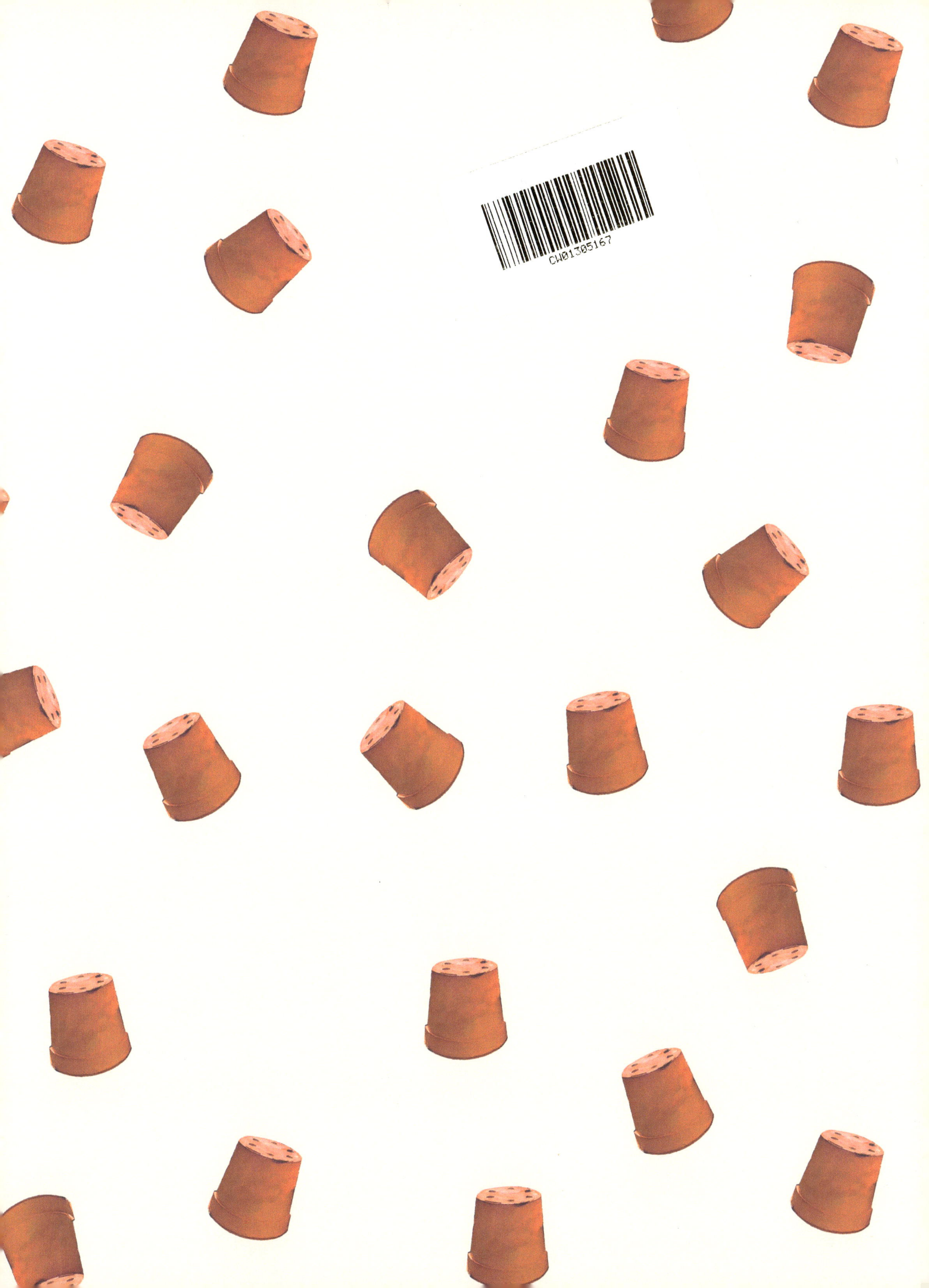

Text and illustrations copyright © 2023 Caroline Seignot
The right of Caroline Seignot to be identified as the author
of this work has been asserted.

All rights reserved. No part of this book may be reproduced, transmitted
or stored in an information retrieval system in any form or by any means,
(graphic, electronic or mechanical, including photocopying, recording
or otherwise) without prior written permission from the Author.

ISBN: 9798857197240

Caroline Seignot

The Donkey And His Drummer

A little boy picked up some sticks,

and he started to drum.

The music danced in his heart so he started to run.

He ran down the lane and into
a farm, with his drumsticks under
his arm.

He passed a stable yard with little regard, but then saw a donkey who was looking quite glum.

The long
eared
fellow
was sad
and in need
of a
chum.

He put down his drumsticks to tickle the donkey under the chin.

Which made the donkey **happy**

so he started to grin.

As the boy walked away, the donkey hopped on to the bench and then over the fence

And he started to march along, as he followed the little boy's song.

They met a cow
by a plough
just
chewing her
cud.

So he started to drum
with a BANG and a THUD!

"You can't drum here, so off you go, this is no place to drum you know!"

Marching on through the meadow, he drummed up high in the air, as a grasshopper jumped in despair!

They found a
sheep who was asleep,
so he drummed
on the fence.

The sheep woke up all cross
and tense.

"You can't drum here, so off you go, this is no place to drum you know!"

Up and down hills they marched further on, in search of a friend to share their song.

They met a duck
with no luck,

as she
was
far
from
the pond.

So he pulled out his drumstick...

...like a
MAGIC WAND!

"You can't drum here, so off you go!

This is no place to drum you know!"

They followed a path tapping his sticks on the trees, as their leaves danced in the summer breeze.

They found a frog on a
log, all wrinkly and green,

and thought to themselves,
"Perhaps he might be keen?"

But alas he was not, and he sounded quite mean!

"You can't drum here, so off you go, this is no place to drum you know!"

They passed a girl on her horse,

who believed in their song.

She pointed to the village,
and told them to,

"Carry on!"

Hearing their song, as they passed by her cottage, a lady told them to,

"STOP!"

As she had made them a drum,

out of a flower pot.

The Donkey and his Drummer rode on to the village, to see a party in full swing. The Nation were celebrating the new King.

As the little drummer boy played his song, the people began to cheer!

A little robin flew down and whispered in his ear.

"You can drum here, so now you know, this is the place to drum you know!"

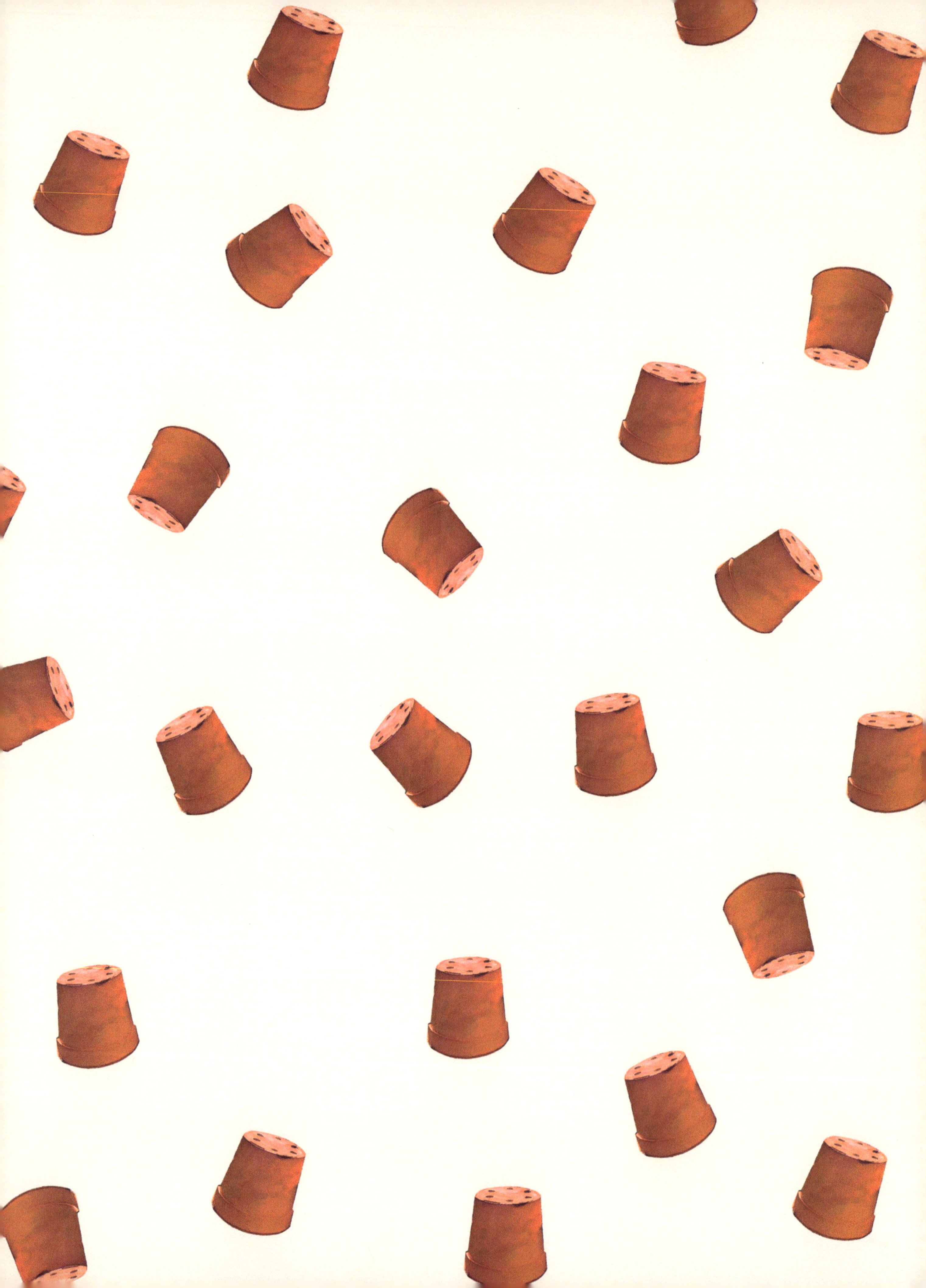

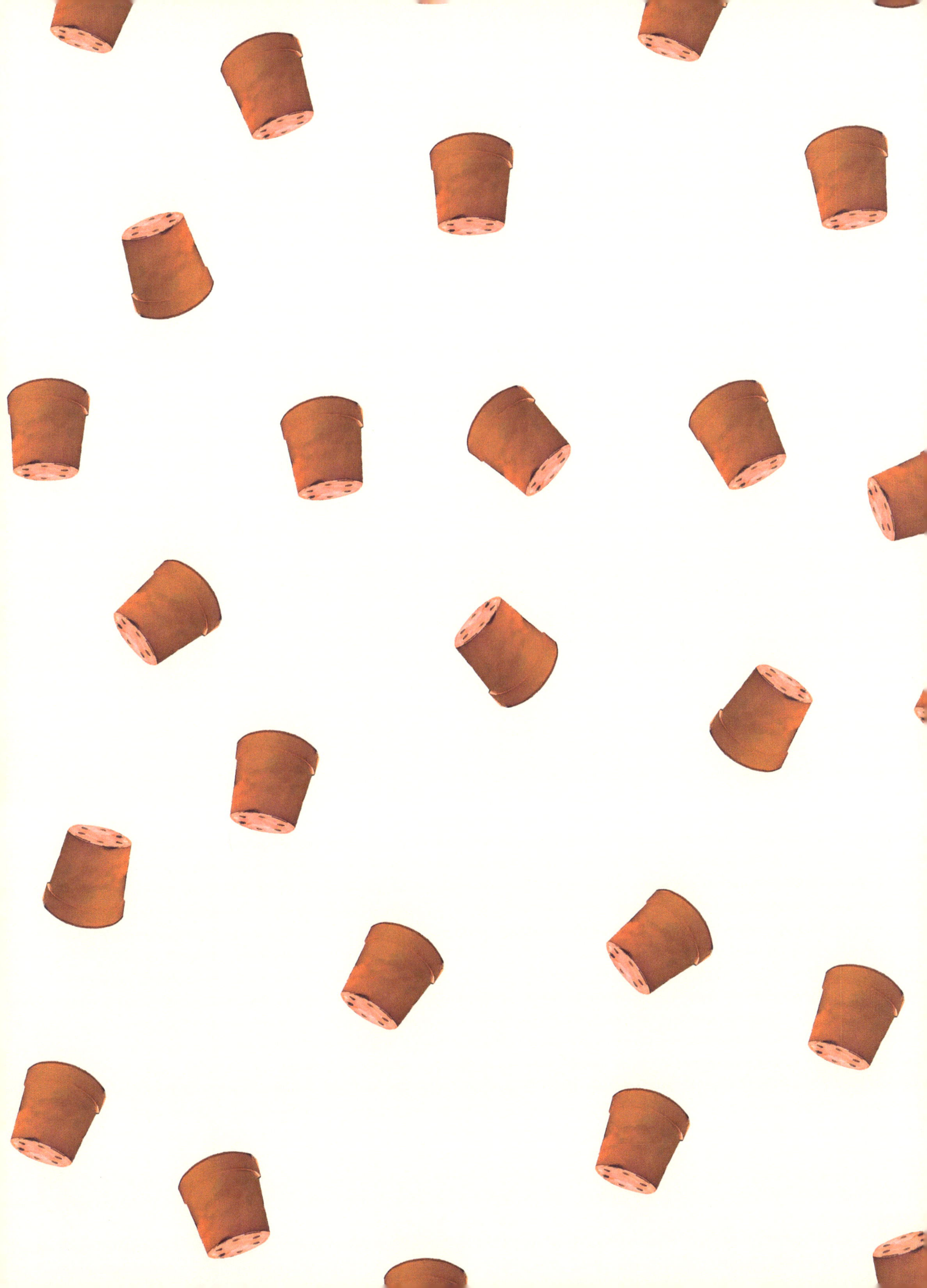